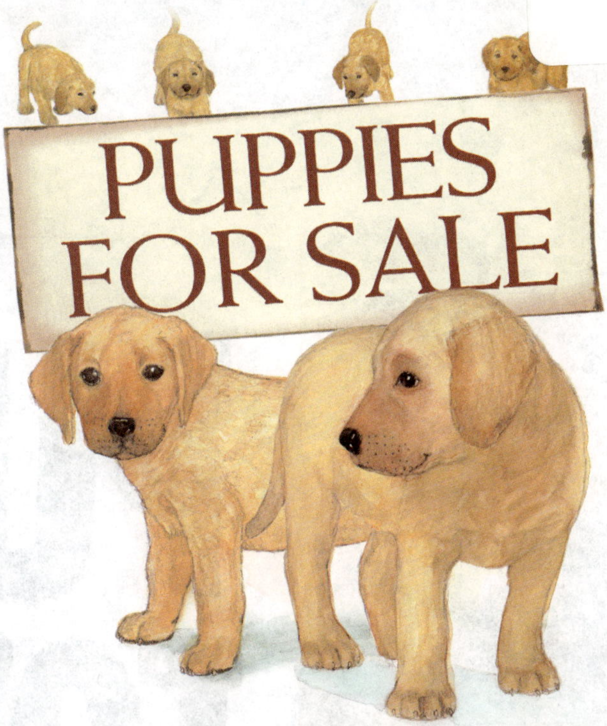

WRITTEN BY DAN CLARK
ILLUSTRATED BY JERRY DILLINGHAM

Published in 2006 in the U.S.A. by Dalmatian Press, LLC
Printed in the U.S.A.

ISBN: 1-40372-984-0
16128/1006 Puppies for Sale

06 07 08 09 NGS 10 9 8 7 6 5 4 3 2 1

PUPPI
FOR SA

A store owner

was tacking a

sign in his store

window which read

PUPPIES FOR SALE,

when a little

boy appeared.

"How much are you selling the puppies for?" he asked.

The man told the lad he didn't expect to let any of them go for less than fifty dollars.

The boy

reached in his

pocket, pulled

out some change,

looked up at the

store owner and

said, "I have two

dollars and thirty-

seven cents.

Can I look at them?"

The store owner

smiled and whistled.

From the kennel,

a dog named Lady

came running down

the aisle, followed

by five tiny

balls of fur.

One puppy

lagged behind.

Immediately,

the little boy

asked about the

limping puppy.

"What's wrong

with the doggie?"

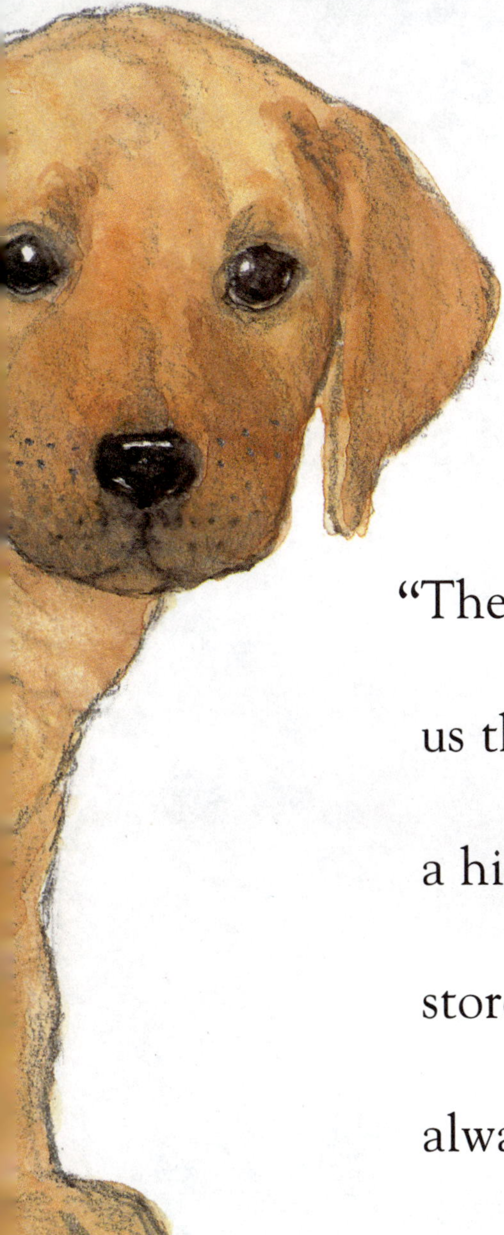

"The veterinarian told us the dog is missing a hip socket," said the store owner. "He'll always limp like that."

“That’s the one

I want to buy,”

the lad said quickly.

The store owner

replied, "No, you

don't want to

buy that dog. If

you really want

him, I'll just give

him to you."

The boy came close to the store owner's face and said angrily, "I don't want you to just give him to me.

That doggie is worth just as much as
all the other puppies and I'll pay the full price.
In fact, I'll give you two dollars and thirty-seven
cents now and fifty cents a month
until I have him paid for!"

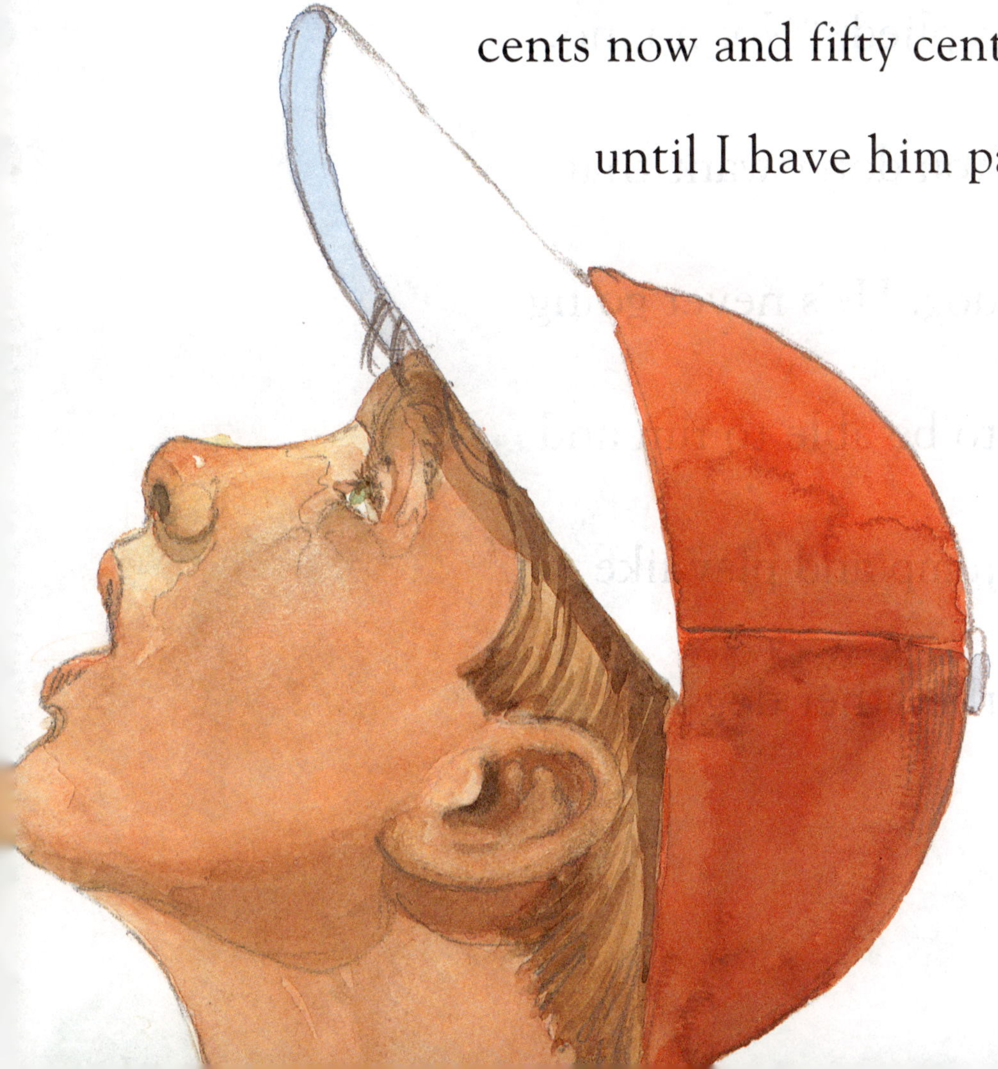

The store owner replied, "No, no, no. You don't want that dog. He's never going to be able to run and jump and play like the other dogs."

In response, the

little boy pulled

up his pant leg

to reveal a badly

twisted right leg,

supported by two

steel braces.

"Well, sir," he said,

"I don't run so well

myself, and the puppy

will need someone

who understands."